For Such A Time...

An endtime call back to the Bible

by
Dan Vis

All Scripture quotations are from the
King James Version of the Bible
Emphasis supplied unless otherwise indicated.

ISBN: 978-0-9821805-0-1

Published by FAST Missions
111 2nd Street
Kathryn, ND 58049

Additional copies of this book are available by
visiting us at WWW.FAST.ST

Dedication

This book is dedicated to David, Rich, Gavin, Josh, Zach, Jin, Jimmy and the rest, whose faithfulness many years ago launched thousands on a journey back to the Bible.

Table of Contents

For Such A Time...
New Preface

This book originally opened with me looking through a chain link fence at the remains of the twin towers, sometime after their destruction on 9/11. I believed then, as I believe now, that this event marked a turning point in prophetic history. It certainly led to a dangerous expansion of assaults on privacy and personal liberty that has persisted from then till now. Like many, I was inspired to study more deeply into endtime events, and became more convinced than ever that God has a special message for His endtime people–revolving around the central importance of His Word. Which led to the initial publication of this book.

Now, on the twenty year anniversary of the twin tower attacks, we are grappling with an even clearer fulfillment of Bible prophecy: thousands of protestors, predominantly Christian, with many sporting Christian flags, banners, and other "Jesus" paraphernalia, launched a violent invasion of the U.S. Capital building, chanting death to certain elected officials, in hopes of overturning election results. Regardless of your political views, one can't help but see it as a similarly traumatic event for our nation, and arguably even more dangerous.

Why? Because it clearly demonstrates the growing involvement of church in politics, and the requisite radicalization of Christianity toward violence–both of which are predicted in the book of Revelation. Sadly, that process is well under way today, with many Christian leaders speaking much more like a dragon, than a lamb already.

And the implications are clearly profound. We are not only twenty years closer to the return of Christ, but we've living in a world where the predicted final scenes are far more conceivable than ever before. And yet, God's endtime people still seem slow to rouse, slow to mobilize, slow to revive. The world has made astonishing progress on its prophetic timeline–yet we seem to have moved no closer to our prophetic destiny.

Which is what this book is all about. It offer a blueprint for the role God's Word will need to play in preparing a people for the crisis just ahead. A blueprint that grows increasingly important with each passing year.

And so it seemed appropriate, to use the twenty year anniversary of the 9/11 attacks to issue a reprint of this book. May the Lord use it to inspire many with the urgency of hiding God's Word in their heart!

For Such A Time...
Original Preface

For years, there has been a growing sense that something is wrong. Long ere this, the work should have been finished–yet time lingers on. Pastors and laymen alike seem almost insensible to the magnitude of the crisis ahead and to the caliber of preparation that will be needed. Deep down we realize there must be some kind of spiritual awakening among our people. But how? What will it take? Are we ever going to see it happen?

This book you hold in your hands contains cutting-edge insights into the Word of God–insights that suggests an unconventional, even radical answer to many vital questions being asked today. The implications are profound.

Jesus is about to come. Even now He is laboring earnestly to bring the great controversy to a close. The final crisis is just ahead–and every man's destiny will soon be decided, forever. All heaven is about to break loose in one last effort to save fallen man. Nothing will be held back. And you and I can be a part. In fact, we are called to be a part.

Yes, God is moving around the world. Men and women everywhere are catching a vision for what God wants to do–and it is burning like a fire in our bones. Allow us to present that vision–*for such a time…*

Behold I Come Quickly
Chapter 1

It is time for thee, LORD, to work:
for they have made void thy law.
Psalms 119:126

The Lord gives a special truth for the people
in an emergency. Who dare refuse to publish it?[1]

My fingers clasped the chain link fence and I pulled myself up onto the narrow concrete ledge for a better view. Thousands, crowding in on either side of me, pressed blank faces into the wire. It was just days after the one year anniversary of the September 11 tragedy, and I found myself staring down into the enormous pit called "ground zero."

Fourteen months earlier, I had been on the East Coast for a family reunion, and had used the opportunity to visit the Statue of Liberty with my family. I remember looking over from Liberty Island to the twin towers punctuating the Manhattan skyline. We had even taken some pictures of them. Now, those towers were gone.

---

1. *Great Controversy, p. 609.*

Somewhere between those two visits, during a layover in New Jersey, I remember glancing across the channel through an airport window and noticing the missing towers. A strange feeling came over me as the reality of the misshapen skyline sunk in. Even so, seeing the disaster site first hand left me dazed. Long minutes passed as I stared into the gaping wound.

Yes, the wreckage had been excavated. Everything was "sanitized" for public viewing. Industrious hawkers had even set up tables to sell 9/11 souvenirs. Manhattan was flourishing. But the empty hole was inescapable: a silent testimony that something had gone wrong.

SOMETHING IS WRONG

Of course, signs our world was heading for trouble have been accelerating for years. I remember a beautiful spring day several years back, while living in Oklahoma. I was using the time to catch up on some things in the garden. Though there was not a cloud in the sky–I suddenly heard the distant rumble of thunder. Others, inside buildings, told me they saw pictures rattling on the wall. The Oklahoma City Federal building had just been destroyed. We felt the blast some 25 miles away!

On another occasion, I was sitting at an airport in Phoenix, Arizona watching the news monitors while waiting for my connecting flight to do a week of prayer on the east coast. Suddenly, a major news story broke out: two disturbed students in Columbine, Colorado had gone to their high school to carry out some deranged fantasy of killing as many classmates as possible, and then taking their own lives. Tragically enough, two years later, I was sitting in that exact same airport, flying to another speaking engagement. And again I was watching the news monitors, trying to catch up on the latest headlines–when suddenly another horror story broke out. This time it was a thirteen year old boy in southern California, who had brought a pistol to school.

EVIDENCE IS EVERYWHERE

Yes, evidence abounds that our world is in trouble. The Middle East simmers with a suicidal hatred toward the West while the Israelis and Palestinians drag out their interminable deadlock. The Cold War shows signs of rekindling, and powder kegs sprinkled around the globe threaten to explode at any moment: North Korea, Venezuela, Kashmir, Taiwan, Tibet, Iran, Kosovo, Somalia. Where will trouble erupt next?

On the economic side, politicians labor in vain to ensure financial stability while the dollar continues to shrink and the national debt continues to expand. Much of the third world is grinding away under oppressive exploitation, causing untold misery: poverty, famine, and disease. All the while, consumers in more prosperous countries, spend billions on debased entertainment filled with violence, sensuality, and ungodly values.

Even the planet seems to be teetering. Environmental devastation is everywhere. Pollution and toxic waste. Global warming. Deforestation. Gigantic ocean dead zones. Bizarre weather patterns. Hurricanes, earthquakes, mud slides and floods, raging fires, tsunamis, and volcanos are all becoming increasingly common. Natural disasters seem to be escalating unlike any period in recorded history.

Most students of Bible prophecy discern clearly that the restraining influence of God's Spirit is gradually being withdrawn from the earth. There's no other explanation.

A SPIRITUAL CRISIS

We are also seeing the dark clouds of an impending spiritual crisis gathering on the horizon. Many evangelical seminaries are riddled with higher criticism, the theory of evolution, and pop psychology–while best-selling books and movies, like the "Left Behind" series, and "The Passion" fill the minds of millions with false conceptions of Bible truth. Every wind of doctrine is blowing. Confusion is rampant.

At the same time, religion is becoming an increasingly potent force in American politics–with both Republicans and Democrats scrambling to highlight their personal commitment to God. And religious leaders are showing an increased willingness to use their positions to influence legislation. A deadly combination for both church and state.

And no longer can we count on the U.S. Supreme Court to provide much protection to religious minorities. The last Chief Justice argued: "the wall of separation between church and state … has proved useless as a guide to judging. It should be frankly and explicitly abandoned." Interestingly enough, the nomination of Judge Alito to the supreme court, creating what will be the first Catholic majority on the Supreme Court in this country's history, was announced on the exact anniversary of Martin Luther's posting of his 95 thesis. The date generally recognized as the birth of the reformation. Those concerned about our crumbling respect for religious freedom are already giving muffled warnings of "extremism," "theocracy," and a "march into fascism." But no one seems to be listening.

Over recent decades the papacy has been growing in power, and begun making calls for the global community to enact "civil legislation" to protect the "sanctity of Sunday worship." And many among the more militant in the Christian right seemed determined to move America that direction.

Interestingly, shortly after 9/11, in a letter written to supporters, the president of the Lord's Day Alliance wrote: "We stand on the verge of an unprecedented opportunity to proclaim the message of the Christian Sunday in a manner unseen at least in my lifetime." The stage, it seems, is all but set. Another crisis or two, and we could soon be facing earth's final test.

WHERE IS GOD?

In my various travels across the country, I have noticed a widespread and growing conviction among believers that time is short. Everywhere, people are expressing an urgent sense of need for a deeper spiritual preparation. And many are growing increasingly troubled by the lack of spirituality in our churches. It is almost as if the unfolding of prophecy taking place around us were some kind of slow motion movie. We sit watching, spellbound–as if powerless to act–while multitudes race on toward destruction. Something is wrong.

Which leads to an important question: where is God? Shouldn't heaven be launching some sort of counter offensive? Shouldn't there be some Spirit-inspired effort to revive and prepare our beloved church for what is just ahead? The enemy is clearly at work, and he is making rapid advances on every front. But what about God? What is heaven doing?

Of one thing we can be sure, heaven is at work. Whenever the moral fabric of society begins to rip apart–God always moves. "It is time for thee, LORD, to work: for they have made void thy law" (Psalms 119:126). The signs in our world give us every reason to believe God is poised to do something special among His people. The more clearly we see Satan's hand in current events, the more certain we can be that God's hand is moving also, somewhere. But we must know where to look.

AN URGENT MESSAGE

In times of trial, God always works through His Word. That is, He raises up individuals to proclaim a special message from Scripture. Notice: "different periods in the history of the church have each been marked by the development of some special truth, adapted to the necessities of God's people at that time."[2] The final crisis will be no different: "amid the confusing cries ... will be borne a special testimony, a special message of truth appropriate for this time."[3]

When it comes to the final crisis, we have the distinct advantage of even knowing what passage of Scripture God will use: "Christ is coming the second time, with power unto salvation. To prepare human beings for this event, He has sent the first second, and third angels' messages."[4] Something about this passage is uniquely powerful. Which is doubtless why God's people are told "the proclamation of the first, second and third angels' messages" is "a work of the most solemn import ... There is no other work of so great importance. They are to allow nothing else to absorb their attention."[5] Clearly God is going to use the words of these three angels in a special way to prepare His church for what is soon to come.

The Bible itself suggests the same thing. In Revelation fourteen, John actually sees, in vision, the "everlasting gospel" going "to every nation, and kindred, and tongue, and people" under the symbolism of these three mighty angels

---

2. *Great Controversy, p. 609.*

3. *Review & Herald, 10/13/1904.*

4. *Bible Commentaries, vol. 7, p. 978-979.*

5. *Last Day Events, p. 45-46.*

(Revelation 14:6). The next few verses give the content of their messages. Then, immediately following, John sees the result: "here is the patience of the saints: here are they that keep the commandments of God, and the faith of Jesus" (Revelation 14:12). The messages have accomplished their work. They have produced at last what the universe has been waiting all these centuries to see: a people who walk in genuine obedience to God through a faith like that of Jesus himself.

SOMETHING IS MISSING

Of course, people have been studying the messages of these three angels for years. They have been preached by thousands, around the globe. We have announced the hour of God's judgment, proclaimed the fall of Babylon, and warned of the mark of the beast. And God has blessed these efforts. No question about it. But can we say these messages have truly prepared a people for the return of Christ–even yet?

Look around you. Are the members in your church fully keeping the commandments of God? Are they genuinely living by the faith of Jesus? Is your church really ready to meet Jesus–right now? If we are honest, most of us would have to admit these messages have not yet fully accomplished their purpose in our own lives! Something is missing.

I believe it is simply that we have failed to completely grasp the meaning of these messages. Or to put it differently: "In these last days, it is our duty to ascertain the *full meaning* of the first, second and third angel's messages."[6] For these messages to do their job, there must be more we need to understand!

Fortunately, it is predicted this time of deeper

---

6. *Last Day Events, p. 68.*

understanding would eventually come: "the fourteenth chapter of Revelation is a chapter of the deepest interest. This scripture *will soon be understood* in all its bearings, and the messages given to John the revelator will be repeated with distinct utterance."[7] These words, penned long after the main prophetic symbols in these verses had been largely unraveled, point forward to a future time when God would give his people even deeper insights into their meaning. Fresh insights would come to the surface that would so electrify the workers, they would be driven to repeat the good news everywhere–with "distinct utterance."

Are we entering the closing scenes of earth's history? Then we can be confident God is working. And specifically, we can expect Him to be giving His people a deeper understanding of a particular passage of Scripture: the three angels messages of Revelation fourteen. An understanding calculated to strengthen us for the final crisis. Insights that will prepare us at last to meet Christ in peace. Insights desperately needed right now.

Could it be that time is here? That the stage really is all but set for the final crisis? That we really do stand on the brink of eternity? If so, we can be confident God is at work for His people. Let's eagerly anticipate God's promised blessing as we study afresh the three angels messages. Let's expect God to give us an urgent message–*for such a time...*

---

7. *Review & Herald, 10/13/1904.*

The Fear of the Lord
Chapter 2

Stablish thy word unto thy servant,
who is devoted to thy fear.
Psalms 119:38

Some seem to think that if a man has a wholesome
fear of the judgments of God, it is a proof that
he is destitute of faith; but this is not so.[8]

I was sitting at a stoplight in northern California, when I first noticed the car behind me. It was a small white sports car, jacked up in the back, and with stripes down the sides. The driver was a spikey-haired teenager, in a leather jacket covered with metal brads and buckles. Then I noticed the sticker plastered across the center of his front bumper: "No Fear."

Interestingly enough, just the weekend before I had been visiting an area church, and had picked up a bumper sticker being given out there. It had since been attached to the center of my rear bumper, right in this young driver's direct line of sight. And the message it shouted? "Fear God."

---

8. *Review & Herald, 10/21/1890.*

His car eventually came to a stop, inches behind mine, giving our two bumper stickers a chance to glare at one another, while we waited for the light to turn green. All of a sudden it struck me: right there on that sunny California street was being acted out the whole great controversy in miniature. Man wanting to go his own way, without any thought or regard to the will of God. And God answering back that we would be wiser if we listened to what He had to say.

Which brings us to the very beginning of God's final warning to planet earth: the three angels messages of Revelation fourteen. The messages destined to produce a people who will finally "keep the commandments of God, and the faith of Jesus." Notice how the passage starts: "And I saw another angel fly in the midst of heaven, having the everlasting gospel to preach unto them that dwell on the earth, and to every nation, and kindred, and tongue, and people, saying with a loud voice, *Fear God...*" (Revelation 14:6-7).

It makes sense, of course, that God would begin such an important message with these words. According to Solomon, "the fear of the LORD is the beginning of knowledge" (Proverbs 1:7). And again, "the fear of the LORD is the beginning of wisdom" (Proverbs 9:10). If the fear of the Lord is the beginning of knowledge and the beginning of wisdom, how could we hope to understand the rest of the passage without it?[9]

Notice also, that this first angel is the one which carries the "everlasting gospel." Evidently this fear of the Lord is somehow connected to the plan of salvation. David put it this way: "the secret of the LORD is with them that *fear him*; and he will shew them his covenant" (Psalms 25:14). The mysteries of

---

9. *It is not only the beginning, but also the conclusion. "Let us hear the conclusion of the whole matter: Fear God, and keep his commandments: for this is the whole duty of man." Ecclesiastes 12:13.*

God's covenant–the Gospel–are evidently only revealed to those who have a living experience in the fear of the Lord. In light of this, where else could the first angel's message begin?

THE FEAR OF THE LORD

The fear of the Lord actually runs through Scripture like a scarlet thread from beginning to end. Take Noah for example: "by faith Noah, being warned of God of things not seen as yet, *moved with fear*, prepared an ark to the saving of his house" (Hebrews 11:7). Noah believed God meant exactly what He said and he acted. The fear of the Lord led to the salvation of his family.

Or think of Abraham. At the very last moment, just before he was to plunge his knife into Isaac on Mount Moriah, a voice cried out from heaven: "Lay not thine hand upon the lad, neither do thou any thing unto him: for now I know that thou *fearest God*" (Genesis 22:12). Abraham's test was on this question of the fear of the Lord. Would he obey God even at the cost of that which was dearest to him in all the world? Destiny hung in the balance.

Even the thief on the cross. When one began mocking Jesus, "the other answering rebuked him, saying, Dost not thou *fear God*?" (Luke 23:40). The fear of the Lord pricked his heart with conviction and won him the promise of eternal life. Yes, there is power in the fear of the Lord.

The topic, however, is not so popular today. We like to speak of God's love, His grace, His mercy. But how often do we dwell on his holiness, his justice, or the fact that there are limits to his forbearance? How often do we really concern ourselves with finding out God's counsel on a given subject? And when we do, how serious are we about complying with His instructions? God's people must give the solemn call to every nation, and kindred, and tongue, and people: fear God. But are we ourselves ready to give that message?

Proverbs tells us much about the fear of the Lord. "The fear of the LORD" it says, "is to hate evil" (Proverbs 8:13). Something about it causes sin to lose its attractiveness, its power to tempt. "The fear of the LORD" it continues, "is a fountain of life, to depart from the snares of death" (Proverbs 14:27). That is, it enables us to detect and escape the subtle traps our enemy sets for our feet. And again: "by the fear of the LORD men depart from evil." (Proverbs 16:6). The fear of the Lord somehow frees us–shattering the shackles of sin in our life, and rendering them powerless. Whatever it is, it works. And we should long for it!

ENTERING THE EXPERIENCE

Fortunately, Proverbs also tells us how to enter into the experience. "My son, if thou wilt receive my words, and hide my commandments with thee…" (Proverbs 2:1). Note the condition: we must open ourselves to His Word and begin storing it in our memory. Writing it on the tables of our heart. Laying it up in our minds. Memorizing it.

But not just memorizing it–memorizing it in a certain way: "So that thou incline thine ear unto wisdom, and apply thine heart to understanding; Yea, if thou criest after knowledge, and liftest up thy voice for understanding; If thou seekest her as silver, and searchest for her as for hid treasures…" (vs 2-4).[10] We must meditate on the Scriptures we memorize. We must cry out to God for insight and understanding. We must take His

---

10. *It is definitely something valuable. According to Isaiah 33:6, "the fear of the LORD is his treasure." And in Proverbs 21:20 we read, "There is treasure to be desired . . . in the dwelling of the wise."*

Word and bring it to bear upon our own personal lives. We must wrestle to know what God is saying to us, individually. We must memorize, yes, but in the way outlined by Scripture.

And the results? "Then shalt thou understand the fear of the LORD, and find the knowledge of God" (vs 5). The conditions are clear. And the promise unequivocal: Memorize God's Word, cry out to Him for understanding, and you will come to know the fear of the Lord, for yourself.

For many years now, we have been proclaiming the three angel's messages. Boldly we have announced the words of the first angel: "Fear God, and give glory to him; for the hour of his judgment is come" (Revelation 14:7). But have we gone far enough? Have we taught our hearers how to enter into the experience?

MEMORIZING SCRIPTURE

Memorizing Scripture, of course, is commanded throughout the Bible. "And these words, which I command thee this day, shall be in thine heart." "Therefore shall ye lay up these my words in your heart and in your soul." "My son, keep my words, lay up my commandments with thee … write them upon the table of thine heart." "Let thine heart retain my words: keep my commandments, and live." "Receive, I pray thee, the law from his mouth, and lay up his words in thine heart." "I will never forget thy precepts: for with them thou hast quickened me." "I will delight myself in thy statutes: I will not forget thy word." (Deuteronomy 6:6, 11:18, Proverbs 7:1,3 4:4, Job 22:22, Psalms 119:93,16).

The New Testament is just as clear, though using slightly different expressions: "Prove all things; hold fast that which is good." "Hold fast the form of sound words." "Behold I come quickly: hold that fast which thou hast." "Let the word of Christ dwell in you richly." "Keep in memory what I preached unto you" (I Thessalonians 5:21, II Timothy 1:13, Revelation 3:11, Colossians 3:15, I Corinthians 15:2). Over and over God urges us to hide Scripture in our heart. We are challenged to give "earnest heed to the things which we have heard, lest at any time we should let them slip" (Hebrews 2:1).[11]

And the connection between the fear of the Lord and God's Word makes sense too. Where Proverbs says the fear of the Lord teaches us to hate evil--Psalms says, "through thy *precepts* I get understanding: therefore I hate every false way" (Proverbs 8:13, Psalms 119:104). Where Proverbs says the fear of the Lord enables us to escape the enemy's snares, Psalms says "thou through thy *commandments* hast made me wiser than mine enemies" (Proverbs 14:27, Psalms 119:98). Where Proverbs says men break free from sin by the fear of the Lord, Psalms says, "Thy *word* have I hid in mine heart, that I might not sin against thee." (Proverbs 16:6, Psalms 119:11). The power, it seems, is in the Bible.

THE WORD AT WORK

Suppose you come home from a hard day at work. You sit back in your favorite armchair, and grab for the remote. Then, just as you get ready to turn on the television, a verse pops into your mind: "turn away mine eyes from beholding vanity; and quicken thou me in thy way" (Psalms 119:37). Your heart is tender, so you surrender to the promptings of the Holy Spirit

---

11. *This is especially true of young people. "God's precious Word is the standard for youth who would be loyal to the King of heaven. Let them study the Scriptures. Let them commit text after text to memory." "The youth who has hidden within the heart and mind a store of God's Words of caution and encouragement, of His precious pearls of promise, from which he can draw at any time, will be a living channel of light." My Life Today, p. 315, Sons & Daughters of God, p. 98.*

– 14 –

and reach for your Bible instead. That is the fear of the Lord!

Or perhaps you are busy washing dishes or some other unpleasant chore, and you catch yourself grumbling under your breath. Immediately a Scripture flashes into your mind: "do all things without murmurings and disputings: that ye may be blameless and harmless, the sons of God without rebuke" (Philippians 2:14-15). You instantly choose to fill your heart with a hymn of praise. The fear of the Lord is at work, again.

Or maybe one morning the alarm goes off, and you find yourself laying there, debating the merits of an extra half hour of sleep. Quietly, the Word calls to your heart: "I love them that love me; and those that seek me early shall find me" (Proverbs 8:17). You roll out of bed and with anticipation, fall on your knees to meet Christ. Once more, it is the fear of the Lord in operation. In each case, it is activated by memorized Scripture.

THE LIFE OF JESUS

Jesus continuously lived His life in this way. The Bible says He was "of quick understanding in the fear of the LORD" (Isaiah 11:3), and it was this that enabled Him to make the choices He did. When we read how Jesus, as a young man, increased "in favor with God and man" (Luke 2:52) we can trace it directly to the sure results of Bible memorization. "Let thine heart keep my commandments … write them upon the table of thine heart: so shalt thou find favour and good understanding in the sight of God and man" (Proverbs 3:1-4). His active memorization of Scripture also enabled him to flawlessly detect, avoid, and overcome all sin. Against each assault of Satan in the wilderness, it was memorized Scripture that gave Christ the victory. In fact, every facet of His life, whether rebuking stubborn priests or training the twelve, was solidly rooted in the

Word of God.[12]

The first angel's message is not just an announcement of the beginning of God's judgment. It is a call to an essential preparation for that judgment. To a moment by moment awareness–through the Word–of God's presence and will for us individually.[13] Proverbs says, "let not thine heart envy sinners: but be thou in the fear of the LORD all the day long" (Proverbs 23:17). How do we go about this? "O how love I thy law! it is my meditation all the day" (Psalms 119:97). It is the internalized Word that will give us this vital experience, and enable us to "give glory to Him" at last.

CONCLUSION

Friend, we need to better understand this fear of the Lord. It is the beginning of knowledge. The beginning of wisdom. It is the key to grasping the secret of the Lord, and His covenant. The fear of the Lord causes us to hate sin, escape its snares, and break its power in our lives. We experience it as we learn to hide God's Word in our heart, and meditate on it through the day–crying out to God for personal applications to our life. It is an essential preparation for God's endtime people. We must get serious about entering into such an experience–*for such a time...*

---

12. *It was also the center of his ministry efforts. "All that was done and said [by Jesus] had this one object in view–to rivet truth in their minds that they might attain everlasting life." Selected Messages, vol. 1, p. 187.*

13. *"The Word of the Living God is not merely written, but spoken. It is God's voice speaking to us just as surely as if we could hear it with our ears. If we realized this, with what awe we would open God's Word, and with what earnestness we would search its pages." Review & Herald, 3/31/1903.*

The Wine of Babylon
Chapter 3

*Thou hast trodden down all them
that err from thy statutes.
Psalms 119:118*

*So closely will the counterfeit resemble the true
that it will be impossible to distinguish
between them except by the Holy Scriptures.[14]*

In November of 1978, the world was shocked by reports of a mass suicide deep in the jungles of Guyana. Over 900 men, women, and children had been ordered to drink cyanide-laced kool-aid at the instruction of a cultic religious leader by the name of Jim Jones. Many were convinced this "miracle working" advocate of social and racial justice was nothing less than an incarnation of Christ himself. Unfortunately, it soon became obvious to the entire world that they had been following the wrong man. He turned out to be another *dead end*.

Jesus warned us, of course, that there would be a dramatic increase in errors and deception just before His return.

---

14. *Great Controversy*, p. 593.

"There shall arise false Christs, and false prophets, and shall shew great signs and wonders; insomuch that, if it were possible, they shall deceive the very elect" (Matthew 24:24). Not only would there be false teachers–but false signs and wonders would attend them. Everything from crying statues to cripples leaping out of wheelchairs. Anyone up on current events knows we are living in such times today.

The apostle Paul similarly warned of deception in the last days. He wrote, "now the Spirit speaketh expressly, that in the latter times some shall depart from the faith, giving heed to seducing spirits, and doctrines of devils" (I Timothy 4:1). Evil angels, he predicted, would gain increased control over the minds of endtime religious teachers, and introduce seductive, false doctrines like never before. Is it happening?

In another place, Paul made a similar statement: "the time will come when they will not endure sound doctrine; but after their own lusts shall they heap to themselves teachers, having itching ears; and they shall turn away their ears from the truth, and shall be turned unto fables" (II Timothy 4:3-4). It is almost as if he is predicting the people of the world would fall under some sort of satanic spell at the end of time, affecting even their desire for truth. Has that time come?

BABYLON IS FALLEN

It is to this point exactly that Revelation fourteen's second proclamation is addressed: "and there followed another angel, saying, Babylon is fallen, is fallen, that great city, because she made all nations drink of the wine of the wrath of her fornication" (Revelation 14:8). Mystery Babylon, that great apostate religious system at the end of time, has fallen from truth--irreversibly. She is condemned for intoxicating, it seems, the entire world with the wine of false doctrine. The second angel's message is an urgent, and impassioned warning against last day deception.

Even a cursory glance at our world today illustrates the timeliness of the warning. Cults and sects of every stripe are proliferating. New age bookstores are in every major city, and their teachings have permeated society. Even the mainline churches seem to be riddled with unbelief: the acceptance of evolution, the denial of inspiration, the ordination of homosexuals, and more. Not so long ago I remember visiting a local Christian book store, and was shocked to see a prominent display in the center of the store advocating the latest book. Its title? "Finding the Lord in the Lord of the Rings." As if sorcery and magic could be an allegory for truth! What is happening to Christianity?

Perhaps a more important question, what is the cause? Just what is it that has made modern day churches so susceptible to devilish deceptions? What is the mysterious power behind Babylon's seductive appeals?

THE LOVE OF THE TRUTH

The answer can be found in Paul's second letter to the Thessalonians. Here one reads of that great mystery of iniquity, the Antichrist power, already at work in Paul's day and destined for destruction at the second coming of Christ. We also find here the secret to its power: that his "coming is after the working of Satan with all power and signs and lying wonders, and with all deceivableness of unrighteousness in them that perish *because they received not the love of the truth,* that they might be saved" (II Thessalonians 2:9-10). Note that it is the love of truth that inoculates us against error, not just a knowledge of it.

The urgency of recapturing a love for truth can be clearly seen in the following statement: "only those who have been diligent students of the Scriptures and who have received *the love of the truth* will be shielded from the powerful delusion that takes the world captive."[15] A superficial familiarity with Bible truth, and mere intellectual assent is not enough. There must be a diligent searching of the Scriptures, driven by a fervent longing to know what God's Word really teaches. Trusting in our knowledge of the Bible–while destitute of a genuine love for truth–will ultimately leave us unprotected. A precarious position in light of the times we now live in!

We are blessed today with an abundance of Bibles–and powerful tools to study them effectively. Computer software, commentaries, lexicons and concordances, and so on. We have virtually unrestricted access to the Word. Yet somehow, simultaneously, the study of doctrines has become rather unpopular. We have lost our zeal for the genuine, distinctive teachings of Scripture. We have lost that drive to know truth, at any cost.[16] We have lost that sense of urgency to acquire a solid understanding of the Scriptures. And now, when truth is more important than ever, it is quietly slipping from our grasp.

THEOLOGICAL PLURALISM

Even in our own beloved church, there is growing confusion. Every wind of doctrine, it seems, is blowing. Theologians wrangle endlessly, each attracting their own small core of followers, while the remaining members throw up their hands in despair–convinced truth is too complicated to be worth the trouble. Not so many years ago a popular writer interviewed

---

15. *Great Controversy, p. 625.*

16. *"Study your Bible as you have never studied it before. Unless you arise to a higher, holier state in your religious life, you will not be ready for the appearing of our Lord." Testimonies for the Church, vol. 5, p. 717.*

five different well known speakers about their understanding of the Gospel, and published his findings in a book. By the end of the book, only one point remains clear: even on a subject as foundational as the Gospel, no two of the five could agree!

It is almost as if the study of doctrines has become something to avoid in our churches. We talk about the need for a relationship with Christ–but forget that a relationship, to be healthy, must be founded on truth. All too often, we focus on those dwindling few points we hold in common–in hopes of avoiding controversy. And those who bring up theological questions or emphasize the distinctives that set us apart as a people, are often marginalized by being labeled as critical, divisive, or imbalanced. Political correctness all too often trumps even Scriptural correctness. And all the while, the theological integrity of our doctrinal foundations continue to erode piece by piece. It is dangerous to even express concern.

Rather than following Jude's exhortation to "earnestly contend for the faith which was once delivered unto the saints" (Jude 1:3) we are stumbling into theological pluralism. Which is really a lack of spiritual concern about error. When was the last time you saw a group of believers gather together over some divisive issue, open the Scriptures, and actually come to a unified position under the guidance of the Holy Spirit? The reality is, we just don't want to make the effort necessary to be "perfectly joined together in the same mind and in the same judgment" (I Corinthians 1:10). Bottom line: there is a widespread lack of love for truth.

BACK TO THE BIBLE

One day, while I was working at a small college in northern California, a fellow teacher came by to talk with me. He shared how he had been watching from a distance our efforts to awaken an interest in Bible memorization among the young people there, but had not been particularly convicted about his need to get involved himself. Then he shared how he had stumbled across something during family worship that stopped him cold in his tracks. He had wrestled with it for days, and at last surrendered, utterly convicted of his need to begin memorizing. Now he wanted help in getting started. Here is what he had read: "None but those who have fortified the mind with the truths of the Bible will stand through the last great conflict."[17]

What commentary is needed? The message is inescapable. Unless we begin storing our mind with truth–we will find ourselves unprepared for Satan's final deceptions. While Jesus promised the Holy Spirit would "bring all things to your remembrance," we are warned "the teachings of Christ must previously have been stored in the mind in order for the Spirit of God to bring them to our remembrance in the time of peril."[18] Apart from that preparation, not one of us will stand.

Peter said, "be ready always to give an answer to every man that asketh you a reason of the hope that is in you" (I Peter 3:15). Which means we must get back to the Word–back to where the answers are. "Have not I written to thee excellent things in counsels and knowledge ... that thou mightest answer *the words of truth* to them that send unto thee?" (Proverbs 22:20-21). How are we to equip ourselves to give such answers? "It is a pleasant thing if thou *keep them within thee*; for they shall be withal fitted in thy lips" (vs 18). What people want is Scripture, not human opinion. "He that hath my word, let him speak my word faithfully. What is the chaff to the wheat?"

---

17. *Great Controversy, p. 593-594.*

18. *Great Controversy, p. 600. See also John 14:26.*

(Jeremiah 23:28). Or as Isaiah puts it, "if they speak not according to this word, it is because there is no light in them" (Isaiah 8:20). The answers are there in Scripture. We just need to start hiding them in our heart!

A CANADIAN EXPERIENCE

A few years ago I was invited to Canada to do a weekend retreat in one of the western provinces. Near the end of the weekend, a special service was planned for praise and testimonies. I doubt anyone there will forget one particularly moving testimony shared that night.

A middle aged woman began by describing how months earlier she had begun feeling increasingly convicted of the need to get back to the Scriptures. It was not that she had anything against books by other Christian writers; rather, it was that something inside her was crying out for *God's* Word. Yet when she shared this burden with her pastor and various church friends, she found her ideas rejected as "narrow-minded," "extreme," and "overly negative." With tears streaming down her face, she described how she had grown discouraged, and eventually fell into despair. Why could no one else understand what she was saying? Was she completely misguided? Or worse, deceived? What was so wrong with simply wanting more of the Bible? Gradually, she began "missing" church on occasion and considered giving up on Christianity altogether.

One day a friend invited her to the retreat I was conducting, and as it was going to be on the importance of God's Word, she reluctantly agreed to come. Deep down, she feared it would be just another disappointment. And if it was, she vowed, she would never step foot in a church again!

Because she arrived late Friday night, her first meeting was an early morning prayer session the next day. That speaker, an area pastor, started by holding up a trendy book popular among evangelicals at the moment, and encouraged his listeners to read it. Her heart sank. It wasn't what she drove all those miles to hear! She started to get up and leave right then and there, and was only barely persuaded by her friend to stay. She would stick around for one more meeting–and no more.

The rest of the day I spoke earnestly on the absolute importance of God's Word–especially in light of the times in which we live. Not knowing any of her story, I shared how the three angels messages were an urgent call back to the Bible. It was just what she had been sensing herself, and it touched a responsive chord. Peace flooded her heart–she had not been deceived! Jesus was indeed coming soon. We do need a love for Scripture.

CONCLUSION

It wasn't so many years ago, our people were well-known for being "the people of the book." Nowadays, though, what I mostly hear is how we *used to be* a people of the book. We little resemble any longer the great protestant reformers of the sixteenth century: Luther, and Calvin, and Huss, willing to lay their lives on the line for some point of *doctrine*. But God needs such men and women today! When our grasp of truth is soon to be tested like no generation before, we are losing our love for it. The trend must be reversed. We must regain our reputation once more.

There is only one way: you must "study to shew thyself approved unto God, a workman that needeth not to be ashamed" (II Timothy 2:15). We must "prove all things" and "hold fast that which is good" (I Thessalonians 5:21). Almost irresistible deceptions lie just ahead. Our only protection is to begin fortifying our mind with Scripture and, with all love and kindness, "contend for the faith" entrusted to us (Jude 1:3). We must plead for a genuine love for truth–*for such a time...*

Whom Will Ye Serve?
Chapter 4

I have inclined mine heart to perform
thy statutes alway, even unto the end.
Psalms 119:112

The Savior desired to fix the faith of his followers
on the word. When His visible presence should be
withdrawn, the word must be their source of power.[19]

I don't know if the same commercials still run on television today, but I remember one particular ad from my childhood years. It would start with a bunch of mechanical stuffed bunnies all moving around together. One by one they begin to loose power and grind to a halt in their movements, until one sole survivor is seen marching off into the sunset. As the camera pans around, you notice the plate on its back is missing, making the brand of battery inside conspicuously noticeable. The point was simple–while everything might look the same on the outside, the secret to success in the long run depends on the *power source* inside. It is a good point to keep in

---

19. *Desire of Ages*, p. 390.

mind as a Christian.

Though one might not see the connection at first, that old commercial illustrates the heart of the third angel's message: "And the third angel followed them, saying with a loud voice, If any man worship the beast and his image, and receive his mark in his forehead, or in his hand, the same shall drink of the wine of the wrath of God, which is poured out without mixture into the cup of his indignation" (Revelation 14:9-10).

What a terrifying thought: God's wrath "unmingled" with mercy poured out on those who receive the mysterious mark. And what does this have to do with batteries?

THE MARK VS THE SEAL

To begin with, one should note the third angel's message is really a call to a choice: between the mark of the beast and the seal of God. Every living person will ultimately be forced to choose between one or the other. The only way to avoid the mark of the beast is to receive the seal of God. Fail to get the seal, and you will end up with the mark. It's just that simple. The third angel's message is thus an echo of Joshua's old challenge: "choose you this day whom will ye serve" (Joshua 24:15). It is one or the other. There is no in-between.

The seal of God is intimately connected with God's law. In Isaiah 8:16, we read, "bind up the testimony, seal the law among my disciples." And it is not limited to one particular part of the law. "For whosoever shall keep the whole law, and yet offend in one point, he is guilty of all." "Man shall not live by bread alone, but by every word that proceedeth out of the mouth of God. (James 2:10, Matthew 4:4). No practicing thief or adulterer can have the seal of God regardless of how conscientious they may be in keeping the Sabbath or abstaining from idolatry. All of the precepts in God's law are intricately interconnected. And we need all of them stamped into our hearts.

Of course, having this law written in the heart has been God's plan all along. "But this shall be the covenant that I will make with the house of Israel; After those days, saith the LORD, I will put my law in their inward parts, and write it in their hearts" (Jeremiah 31:33). The seal of God, put simply, is His Word stamped so firmly into the mind and heart, that it transforms the character and controls the life. So deeply that it makes an imprint that endures for eternity. "The office of the Holy Spirit is to take the truth from the sacred page, where God has placed it ... and stamp that truth upon the mind."[20]

There is power in the Scriptures. The Bible says we are "born again, not of corruptible seed, but of incorruptible, by the word of God, which liveth and abideth for ever" (I Peter 1:23). Through God's promises we can become "partakers of the divine nature, having escaped the corruption that is in the world through lust" (II Peter 1:4) and "cleanse ourselves from all filthiness of the flesh and spirit, perfecting holiness in the fear of God." (II Corinthians 7:1). Talk about power!

But like any seed it must be planted. It must be given time to root down into our lives if it is to accomplish its work. We must "receive with meekness the engrafted word, which is able to save [our] souls" (James 1:21). Grafting takes time. God's Word must be thoroughly intertwined into who and what we are.

---

20. *Health Living, p. 300. Elsewhere we read, "it is not any seal or mark that can be seen, but a settling into the truth, both intellectually and spiritually, so they cannot be moved." Last Day Events, p. 219-220.*

RIGHTEOUSNESS BY FAITH

This, of course, is what true righteousness by faith is all about. Today it seems there are more animated discussions about this particular theological phrase than just about any other. And there are nearly as many theories on the subject as there are teachers! Yet the Bible is surprisingly clear. It defines what righteousness by faith is precisely:

> *But the righteousness which is of faith speaketh on this wise, Say not in thine heart, Who shall ascend into heaven? (that is, to bring Christ down from above:) Or, Who shall descend into the deep? (that is, to bring up Christ again from the dead.) But what saith it? The word is nigh thee, even in thy mouth, and in thy heart: that is, the word of faith, which we preach. Romans 10:6-8*

There it is. True righteousness by faith is simply laying hold, by faith, on the power of the internalized Word to produce real righteousness. After all, faith that is not directly rooted in the Bible is not faith at all–it is presumption. As Paul pointed out just a few verses later: "so then faith cometh by hearing, and hearing by *the word of God*" (Romans 10:17). Yes, righteousness must be rooted in Scripture.[21] That's the power source. It's the only battery that lasts.

---

21. *"Temptations often appear irresistible because through neglect of prayer and the study of the Bible, the tempted one cannot readily remember God's promises and meet Satan with the Scripture weapons." "Those who make the Word their study are arming themselves with weapons of divine power against the attacks of the foe. 'Thy word,' said the Psalmist, 'have I hid in mine heart, that I might not sin against thee.'"* Great Controversy, p. 600, Signs of the Times, 3/9/1882.

Of course, we have a part to play in accessing that power. Proverbs tells us "My son, keep my words and lay up my commandments with thee ... Bind them upon thy fingers, write them upon the table of thine heart" (Proverbs 7:1,3). Paul similarly wrote: "Moreover, brethren, I declare unto you the gospel which I preached unto you, which also ye have received, and wherein ye stand; By which also ye are saved, if ye keep in memory what I preached unto you" (I Corinthians 15:1-2). Our part is to hide God's Word in the heart. God's part is to stamp it into the character.

THE BIBLE ALONE

In the year 1888 at an important religious conference being held in Minneapolis, two young men from the west coast were invited to share some unconventional views on the subject of righteousness by faith to the assembled delegates. Some of the more established brethren began to resist the messages and an angry controversy erupted that continues to this date in some circles. Interestingly enough, right in the midst of the crisis, a little old lady penned the following words, which should have settled the question once and for all:

> *The Bible, and the Bible alone, laid up in the heart and blessed by the Spirit of God, can make a man right and keep him right.*[22]

She pointed them back to the Bible as the only true power source for life-transformation. Our work is to lay it up in the heart, and the Spirit's work is to bless it with supernatural

---

22. *1888 Materials, p. 194.*

energy. Exactly what Paul called righteousness by faith![23] How desperately we need to get back to a Bible-centered conception of righteousness by faith!

THE REAL QUESTION

The real question in the choice between the mark and the seal is quite simple. It is not a hypothetical discussion of how we will respond in some future time of trouble, but rather how we are responding to the various trials and perplexities we face right now. What are we conforming to day by day? The Word of God? Or the world? It is the little choices we make daily that determine our destiny at last.

Notice: "Those who are uniting with the world are receiving the worldly mold and preparing for the mark of the beast. Those who are distrustful of self, who are humbling themselves before God and purifying their souls by obeying the truth–these are receiving the heavenly mold and preparing for the seal of God in their foreheads."[24]

What we usually think of as the mark or seal is really just the final stamp revealing a life-long pattern of decisions. The choice we make then will only *reveal* the choices we are making today. Again, "the time is not far distant when the test will come to every soul ... The contest will be between the commandments of God and the commandments of men. Those who have yielded

---

23. This was also the message of the two young men from the west coast. One of them, A. T. Jones, for example, wrote: "In the Christian life everything depends upon the word of God. It is true that God is able and desires to keep us from sinning, but this must be done through His word. So it is written, 'By the word of thy lips I have kept me from the paths of the destroyer.' 'Thy word have I hid in my heart that I might not sin against thee.' This is the way that God has appointed and there is no other way to have this thing accomplished." Review & Herald, 10/13/1896.

24. The Faith I Live By, p. 288.

step by step to worldly demands and conformed to worldly customs will then yield to the powers that be."[25]

In light of this solemn fact, shouldn't we be more serious about bringing every area of our life into harmony with the Word? Our marriages? our parenting? our employment? our relationships? our entertainment? our lifestyle? The list goes on and on.

A GLORIOUS GOSPEL

Friends, we must not underestimate the power of the Gospel. According to Peter, it offers us "all things that pertain unto life and godliness" and through its "exceeding great and precious promises" we are to become "partakers of the divine nature" (II Peter 1:3-4). Startling words, but words that cannot fail. God says: "so shall my Word be that goeth forth out of my mouth; it shall not return unto me void, but it shall accomplish that which I please, and it shall prosper in the thing whereto I sent it" (Isaiah 55:11). Soon, God will have that people who reflect His character to the world.

What will it take to produce this final generation? Basically, a people who finally give Scripture absolute authority in their life. We must yield on every point. The Bible alone must reign supreme. We must live lives so surrendered, that we instantly respond to the slightest whisper of the Holy Spirit speaking to us through the Scriptures. Learning this kind of responsiveness, of course, takes time. It is a process. A process we cannot afford to put off starting.

---

25. *Lift Him Up, p. 164.*

CONCLUSION

For years I assumed the three angels messages were addressed primarily to those unfamiliar with the great prophetic truths we have loved and cherished so long. And for 160 years we have been proclaiming them as if their primary application was to others: The hour of His judgment has begun! Babylon's deceptions are everywhere! Don't get the mark of the beast! Preaching these messages in such a way has led thousands into a closer walk with Christ. And we must continue to proclaim these vital Bible-based warnings to the world. But there is more.

There is a message in these verses for *us*. And it is exactly what we need at this critical moment in earth's history, to strengthen us for what lies ahead. These messages not only warn a world, but they prepare a people. They call us, as God's children into such an experience in the fear of the Lord that sin's power is shattered in our life. Into such a love for truth that the deceptions of the enemy lose their hold. And perhaps most important of all, into such authentic righteousness by faith that the character of Christ is reproduced in His people. Three power-packed messages, each containing vital principles perfectly calculated to revitalize and ready God's people for Christ's return.

The three angel's messages are an urgent call back to the Bible. To hiding God's Word in our heart–that we might learn the fear of the Lord. To the diligent fortification of our mind with Scripture–driven by a passionate love for truth. And to living by the Bible laid up in the heart and blessed by the Spirit–genuine righteousness by faith. Simply put, to face the final crisis ahead, we must become saturated with God's Word. We must be so filled with Scripture that Bible verses pulse through our veins and arteries. Nothing less will do–*for such a time...*

It's Time for Rain
Chapter 5

I will never forget thy precepts:
for with them thou hast quickened me.
Psalms 119:93

Those who do the work of the Lord ... must close and bolt
the doors firmly against excitement and fanaticism.
The Word of God is our sanctification.[26]

Sometimes it seems we are willing to try almost anything, in hopes of working up a little excitement. It's not uncommon these days to hear of gospel clowns, gospel puppeteers, gospel jugglers, and the like. I even heard once of a Christian grade school who brought in a gospel magician to do a week of prayer. Honestly, a gospel magician?

Others compromise the message by mixing it with worldly music in an attempt to reach our youth. Or they use drama, or dance. Unfortunately such efforts do little to rescue our youth from the powerful pull of the world. If anything, it reinforces their taste for the world, and strengthens its hold on

---

26. *Evangelism, p. 138.*

their life. Most of us would readily admit such "gospel gimmicks" will never bring in revival. At least not *genuine* revival.

Such tactics often stem from misconceptions about the Holy Spirit. For while it's true "a revival of true godliness among us is the greatest and most urgent of all our needs"[27] we must be very careful to not "encourage a spirit of enthusiasm that brings zeal for awhile, but soon fades away, leaving discouragement and depression."[28] What we need is a Bible-based understanding of revival!

THE LATTER RAIN

This is especially true of the latter rain–that great final revival that empowers God's people to actually finish the work. It is a topic we have talked about for years. We have all heard sermons, read articles and books, or attended study groups discussing it–and we have probably prayed for it, as well. Through Joel, God promised "I will pour out my spirit upon all flesh" (Joel 2:28). Through Isaiah, God said "I will pour my spirit upon thy seed, and my blessing upon thine offspring" (Isaiah 44:3). And again through Ezekiel, "I will put my spirit within you, and cause you to walk in my statutes" (Ezekiel 36:27). Many other verses likewise point to a great future time of spiritual refreshing.

Imagine: "a great movement, a work of revival going forward in many places" with people "moving into line, responding to God's call."[29] "Servants of God, with their faces

---

27. *Last Day Events, p. 189.*

28. *Evangelism, p. 138.*

29. *Last Day Events, p. 58.*

lighted up and shining with holy consecration hasten from place to place to proclaim the message from heaven. By thousands of voices all over the earth, the warning is given."[30] It's going to happen.[31]

Yes, this great, long-anticipated, endtime revival is coming, and soon. A powerful awakening is going to sweep through the church, gripping sleepy believers, and arousing thousands to action. And it will spread everywhere, around the globe. The latter rain will be unbelievably exciting. And we are on the verge of it. We have to be.

GOD'S BIG SURPRIZE

But shocking as it sounds, when the latter rain finally comes, many will fail to even notice anything has happened! We've been waiting for it for years. Praying for it. Anticipating it. Reading, studying, and preaching about it. Yet somehow, when it comes at last, many don't even notice? Listen: "Only those who are living up to the light they have will receive greater light. Unless we are daily advancing in the exemplification of the active Christian virtues, *we shall not recognize* the manifestations of the Holy Spirit in the latter rain. It may be falling on hearts all around us, but *we shall not discern* or receive it."[32] How could this be?

The root problem, again, is our dim understanding of how God works. Much like the person using rock music, or a gospel

---

30. *Last Day Events, p. 203.*

31. *"There will soon be an awakening that will surprize many. Those who do not realize the necessity of what is to be done will be passed by, and the heavenly messengers will work with those that are called the common people, fitting them to carry the truth to many places." Last Day Events, p. 204.*

32. *Last Day Events, p. 195-196.*

magician to bring in revival, our expectations are confused. In particular, I would like to suggest there are two common misconceptions about the latter rain that will hinder many from recognizing it.

TWO DIFFERENT RAINS

One common misconception is the belief that there is no real difference between the early and latter rain. We acknowledge, of course, that the latter rain will be more powerful, and more global in extent—but assume that otherwise the two are basically indistinguishable. I've heard more than one church leader talk about the early and latter rain as if there were no real difference between them. But is this what the Bible teaches?

Actually, according to the book of Joel, when the latter rain begins to be poured out, the early rain is poured out *with it.* If there were no difference between the two, why would we need both at the same time? Notice: "Be glad then, ye children of Zion, and rejoice in the LORD your God: for he hath given you the former rain moderately, and he will cause to come down for you the rain, the former rain, and the latter rain in the first month" (Joel 2:23).[33] At Pentecost, the church experienced a powerful outpouring of early rain spiritual grace—and she has continued to experience these early rain showers ever since. During the latter rain, these early rain showers will continue, at least for a time. They clearly fall together! Why both?

---

33. *The word "month" is supplied. A more literal translation might be "he will cause to come down for you the rain, the former rain, and the latter rain at the beginning." Amos 9:13 seems to be an allusion to this time, when both sowing and reaping will be taking place together. "Behold, the days come, saith the LORD, that the plowman shall overtake the reaper, and the treader of grapes him that soweth seed."*

SEEDTIME & HARVEST

The following sheds some light: "The 'former rain' was given in the outpouring of the Holy Spirit at the opening of the gospel, to cause the upspringing of the precious seed."[34] That seed, we know, represents the Word of God (Luke 8:11). Jesus had been preaching it with power for three and a half years. And on Pentecost, that seed germinated–resulting in three thousand new believers! It was the upspringing of the precious seed.

But the statement continues: "So the 'latter rain' will be given at its close for the ripening of the harvest." What is the purpose of the latter rain? To ripen the harvest. To bring the plant to fruition. To complete the growth process. One produces germination–the other maturation. Is there a difference? Absolutely.

Notice again: "Under the figure of the early and latter rain that falls in eastern lands at seedtime and harvest, the Hebrew prophets foretold the bestowal of spiritual grace in extraordinary measure upon God's church. The outpouring of the Holy Spirit in the days of the apostles was the beginning of the bestowal of the early or former rain."[35] Pentecost was the beginning of the early rain, and the church has had access to these showers every since. In fact, every time the Word germinates in a person's heart, every time there is a conversion, a spiritual rebirth–it is evidence the early rain is still doing its work. Which is why we should seek an early rain blessing each and every morning–we need a daily conversion. The Word must spring up fresh in our heart every day.

---

34. *Last Day Events, p. 186.*

35. *Acts of the Apostles p. 54-55.*

But the passage goes on, "Near the close of earth's harvest, a special bestowal of God's grace is promised to prepare the church for the coming of the Son of man. This outpouring of the Holy Spirit is likened to the falling of the latter rain." The latter rain comes at the end of time. It is something *special*. Something unique. Something never seen before. It is what ripens the harvest. What strengthens the church for the final crisis. What prepares it to meet Christ. The latter rain will do what the early rain has not been able to do in 2000 years. It produces a generation of believers unlike anything the universe has ever seen. A generation without "spot, or wrinkle, or any such thing ... holy and without blemish" (Ephesians 5:27). How we need this latter rain!

You see, the early rain and the latter rain have two different functions. The early rain produces conversion. It germinates the seed. The latter rain ripens the harvest, bringing it to completion, to maturation. Without the latter rain, there would be no harvest. The early rain can get a plant growing–but without the latter rain, the plant will never fulfil its ultimate purpose. "'Behold, the husbandman waiteth for the precious fruit of the earth, and hath long patience for it, until he receive the early and latter rain.' James 5:7. So the Christian is to wait with patience for the fruition in his life of the word of God ... Our part is to receive God's word and to hold it fast."[36]

WHAT WOULD IT LOOK LIKE?

Suppose someone were receiving the latter rain in your church. What might it look like? Would there be changes in how they eat, and how they dress? How they spend their time, their

---

36. *Christ's Object Lessons, p. 61.*

money, their energy? How they relate to their spouse, their children, their friends and neighbors? How they think? Absolutely! Suppose they sell their home, cash in their retirement, and head off to some deep dark jungle, burning with a passion to share Christ with those who have never heard? Might we label such a person rash? impulsive? imbalanced? or worse? While the latter rain will produce no extremism, it will produce absolute biblical fidelity.[37] A biblical fidelity those who fail to "come up" on every point are likely to resist energetically. Is this perhaps how it could be falling on hearts all around, without us even noticing?

Too many of us are looking primarily for large numbers of conversions as evidence of the latter rain. There will be conversions during the latter rain, of course, but primarily because the early rain is being poured out *with* the latter rain. As God's people begin to partake more and more fully of the Spirit of Christ, they will become ever more bold and compelling in their preaching of the gospel. And thousands will respond. But that is evidence of the early rain. The evidence of the latter rain is changed lives. Men and women who have been thoroughly transformed. Men and women fully ready to meet Christ.

THE CLOSE OF PROBATION

There is a second reason many of us will be caught by surprize when the latter rain comes. And that is, we have failed to recognize the close connection between the latter rain and the close of probation. Let me illustrate it by looking for a moment at the case of Lucifer. His probation has been closed for some

---

37. *"But God will have a people upon the earth who maintain the Bible and the Bible only as the standard of all doctrines and the basis of all reforms."* *Great Controversy, p. 595.*

time. Do you know why? Understanding the answer to this question is vital.

Follow carefully: "As a sinner, man was in a different position from that of Satan. Lucifer in heaven had sinned in the light of God's glory. To him as to no other created being was given a revelation of God's love. Understanding the character of God, knowing His goodness, Satan chose to follow his own selfish, independent will. This choice was *final*."[38] Think about that for a moment. What more could God do to reveal His character, His nature, His heart? Lucifer was one of the covering cherubim–gazing into the Shekinah glory for long ages. There, in the divine presence, Lucifer chose to sin. That choice was final. There was no fuller revelation God could give. Nothing more He could do.

The passage continues: "But man was deceived ... For him there was hope *in a knowledge of God's love*." Perhaps, if man could just gain a clearer glimpse of God's character. If he could be given a more distinct view of what our loving heavenly Father was really like. If the misrepresentations could be swept aside. The false ideas corrected. Maybe, if man could just grasp more fully the truth of who God was, he might decide to repent and return. There is hope for us because the character of God has been partially obscured by Satan's lies.

The situation was similar with the Jewish nation. Daniel prophesied a certain amount of probationary time, would be set apart for his people (Daniel 9:24). Just before that period came to an end, what happened? "the Word was made flesh, and dwelt among us, and *we beheld His glory*" (John 1:14). The national leaders were given a chance to see the true character of God, the principles of Scripture perfectly lived out in human form–and

---

38. *Desire of Ages, p. 761-762.*

they chose to reject it. In mercy, God even gave them a few extra years. Time to see the transformed lives of the apostles. Time to hear their preaching and understand the issues. Time to reflect more fully on their own choices and conduct. But when all was said and done, they still persisted in their determination to turn away, sealing their fate as a nation, forever, in the stoning of Stephen. What more could God do?

A GLOBAL LIGHT BULB

Now think for a moment what will happen when the latter rain is poured out at last, and God's people begin to fully reflect Christ's character all over the earth? When the entire planet is "lightened with His glory," like a giant light bulb, by Spirit-filled believers around the globe? (Revelation 18:1). When the "knowledge of the glory of the LORD" finally covers the earth "as the waters cover the sea"? (Habakkuk 2:14). What will happen when people are confronted with that kind of glory, and still choose to reject the Savior? Will they not be closing their own probation, just as Lucifer did before the Shekinah glory? As the Jewish leaders did when confronted with the glory of Christ?

Somehow we have this idea in the back of our mind that God has got some giant stopwatch ticking away in His hand. When time is up, God yells out: "Ready or not, here I come." It is not like this at all! God is waiting for us. For a people who will fully reveal His character to the world, so that everyone can make an intelligent choice. So they can make an informed, *final* decision. Then, and only then, will probation close.

To put it simply, probation cannot close, until there is a people sprinkled throughout every corner of the globe, who faithfully reflect His character. There must be a living demonstration of the gospel, a living witness "unto all nations;

and then shall the end come" (Matthew 24:14). "Not one is made to suffer the wrath of God until the truth has been brought home to his mind and conscience, and has been rejected."[39] "The work of the Holy Spirit is to convince the world of sin and of righteousness and of judgment" but "the world can only be warned by seeing those who believe the truth sanctified through the truth, acting upon high and holy principles."[40] God needs such a people. The kind of people only the latter rain can produce.

CONCLUSION

The purpose of the latter rain is not primarily conversions, it is Christian maturity. It's not germination, but fruit. There will be conversions–thousands in a day. But they will be the result of God's people partaking more fully of His Spirit, and proclaiming His message with increased power. It will be the result of the early and latter rain being poured out simultaneously. The latter rain, however, is what ripens that harvest. It is what produces that people who fully reflect His character at last. A people who will live by Scripture, and Scripture alone. Don't you long to be in that number?

While the early rain may have started us on our Christian walk, the latter rain will be required to finish it. The latter rain will empower us to grow up "unto the measure of the stature of the fullness of Christ" (Ephesians 4:13). When God has this people, "the earth" will be "lightened with his glory" (Revelation 18:1). And then every person will be called to make their final choice. Only then can probation close.

---

39. *Great Controversy, p. 605.*

40. *Bible Training School, 12/1/1903.*

Revival is not about Gospel gimmicks. It's neither music nor magic. It is about deep conviction and absolute surrender to the Word of God. And until there exists such a surrendered people, sin and suffering must continue. To give the Word of God full sway in our life, is our greatest need–*for such a time*...

Fuel for the Fire
Chapter 6

The entrance of thy words giveth light;
it giveth understanding unto the simple.
Psalms 119:130

The life of God, which gives life to the world, is
in His Word ... It is our only source of power.
Gospel Workers, p. 250

Several years ago our ministry organized a small mission trip to Malaysia. It was my first visit to a Muslim country, and I must confess I was a bit nervous at first. It was less than a year after the terrorist attacks in New York and I suspected Americans were not particularly popular in that part of the world. My suspicions were confirmed when on my first day in the country I nearly bumped into a man coming out of an elevator wearing a t-shirt promoting Osama Bin Laden! He looked as shocked to see me as I was to see him, then he gave a brief glare, and walked off. That was the extent of my interactions with him!

Fortunately, the rest of the mission trip was filled with many positive experiences, and I grew to love the country and its people. The sights and sounds intrigued me, and the various dishes proved wonderfully delicious. Even more important, the young people who came to our meetings were enthusiastic and made serious commitments to memorize Scripture. All in all it was a blessed and successful trip.

On my last night in the country, our hosts took us into town to browse the various street vendors selling trinkets and souvenirs. Not particularly given to those kind of things, I meandered along, simply enjoying my new friendships, and the cool night air. Then, suddenly I stumbled onto a souvenir I knew I had to get. It was a small alabaster looking oil lamp shaped much like those used in Bible times. I had never seen anything quite like it, so I asked my host to negotiate a price and I purchased it. It's sitting here on my desk in front of me even now as I type these words. A reminder of my time in Malaysia.

A TALE OF TEN VIRGINS

It's also a reminder of a particular passage of Scripture that I believe unlocks an important key to understanding the latter rain. In our last chapter we looked at what the latter rain will accomplish. In this chapter we will look at what we must do to experience it. In particular, we will focus in on what may well be the most overlooked preparation for the latter rain. Something that has been hidden in plain sight all along.

It is the parable of the ten virgins. You remember the story. Five were wise and five were foolish. They are all waiting for the bridegroom, and they all fall asleep when his coming takes longer than expected. They all have lamps–like the lamp I purchased in Malaysia–and each sputters out while they sleep. Suddenly, the cry is heard, "the bridegroom cometh; go ye out to meet him" (Matthew 25:6). They all wake up and try to get their lamps burning. The wise succeed, using the extra oil stored in their vessel. But the foolish, too late, realize they have not made adequate preparation. They have no fuel for the fire. And when they run to go buy more, the bridegroom returns and enters into the marriage supper with those who were prepared. And the door is closed–leaving the foolish shut out. A solemn parable indeed.

It's also relevant. Everything in the parable points to the latter rain. There is a great awakening among the virgins (God's people). It takes place just when the bridegroom's return is imminent (the second coming). Those who made the necessary preparation of storing extra oil in their vessels are able to light up the darkness (the glory of God). And there is even the tragic shut door, which seals the fate of the foolish (the close of probation). If there is any passage of Scripture that explains on how to prepare for the latter rain, it would be this one.

DECODING PARABLES

Now before going further, it is a good idea to review the method one uses to interpret parables. According to Paul, "the Holy Ghost teacheth" by "comparing spiritual things with spiritual" (I Corinthians 2:13). That is, the Bible must explain it's own symbols. Parables, like prophecies, are not a matter of "private interpretation" (II Peter 1:20). Rather, we grow in understanding "precept upon precept … line upon line; here a little, and there a little" (Isaiah 28:9-10).

Take the virgins. What do they represent? In Jeremiah, we read "I have likened [symbolized] the daughter of Zion to a comely and delicate woman" (Jeremiah 6:2). Similarly, Paul writes, "I have espoused you [the Corinthian church] to one husband, that I may present you as a chaste virgin to Christ"

(II Corinthians 11:2). In Scripture, then, women are used as a symbol for God's people. Revelation 12 talks of a pure woman, symbolizing a faithful church whereas Revelation 17 talks of a corrupt woman, representing an apostate church. The same process can be used for the other symbols in the parable.

Take the bridegroom for another example. When asked by the Pharisees why His disciples did not fast, Jesus explained: "the bridegroom is with them" now, "but the days will come, when the bridegroom shall be taken from them, and then shall they fast" (Matthew 9:15). Clearly He was referring to Himself. In Ephesians 5:31-32 the mystery of Christ and the church is explained using the allegory of a man and his wife. Similarly, in Romans, Paul writes that we are "married to another, even to him who is raised from the dead" (Romans 7:4). The theme of Christ coming for His bride is repeated in Revelation and elsewhere. Clearly, the bridegroom is Christ. Which shows again that the Bible can interpret itself.

I remember asking myself the question–why do they all fall asleep? Both wise and foolish? Then I stumbled on to this verse: "Slothfulness casteth into a deep sleep" (Proverbs 19:15). Is it possible that some today, having lost that sense of urgency concerning Christ's return–have grown a bit lazy in their devotional life. Become neglectful in Bible study, prayer, and personal obedience? Almost certainly. In fact, most of us would probably live our lives quite differently if we genuinely believed Christ's return were scheduled for later today!

Two other important symbols are the lamp and the vessel. The lamps evidently point to the Word of God: "Thy word is *a lamp* unto my feet, and a light unto my path." "For the commandment is *a lamp*; and the law is light" (Psalms 119:105, Proverbs 6:23). The vessels were small storage containers used to hold an extra supply of fuel. These seem to represent our hearts: "For God, who commanded the light to shine out of darkness, hath shined *in our hearts*, to give the light of the knowledge of the glory of God in the face of Jesus Christ. But we have this treasure *in earthen vessels*" (II Corinthians 4:6-7). In other words, both the wise and foolish virgins had Bibles in their hands–the difference between them was at the heart level. The wise had made some heart preparation that the foolish had not. How vital then that we understand exactly what they did!

THE CRUCIAL SYMBOL

There is one crucial symbol in the parable. Arguably, the whole point of the parable hinges on it–for it is the only difference between the wise and foolish virgins. Both groups are described as virgins. Both wait for the same bridegroom. Both have lamps and vessels. Both fall asleep, and both wake up. There is only one difference between the wise and foolish virgins–the oil. If we fail to grasp the full meaning of this symbol, doesn't it seem likely we might miss the entire point of the parable?

So what does the oil represent? I have asked this question in churches across the country–and the answer is always the same: The Holy Spirit. Certainly the Holy Spirit is involved. Yet when I ask how many believe it is possible to store up an extra supply of the Holy Spirit in their hearts for the future–there is generally silence. What about it? Is it possible to pray extra hard one day and get so much of the Holy Spirit we can afford to skip devotions the next morning? Aren't we supposed to get fresh supplies of the Holy Spirit–*daily*? Yet somehow the wise have stored up extra oil in their vessels. Perhaps there is more to this symbol than we have generally thought.

THE GOLDEN OIL

To better understand this aspect of the parable we must dig a little deeper. We must, as with the other symbols, allow inspired writings to interpret inspired writings. One Old Testament passage involving oil immediately comes to mind: Zechariah 4:11-14. In vision, the prophet sees "two olive trees upon the right side of the candlestick and upon the left side thereof" and "two golden pipes" which "empty the golden oil out of themselves." These olive trees, he is told, "are the two anointed ones, that stand by the Lord of the whole earth." A bit cryptic, admittedly–but we know this much at least: if we want to get oil for our vessels, we must find these two trees. They are the source.[41]

Fortunately our search need not take too long. Revelation calls them by a more familiar name: "And I will give power unto my *two witness* … these are the *two olive trees* … standing before the God of the earth" (Revelation 11:3-4). The two olive trees then, and the two witnesses, must both symbolize the same thing. And whatever that is–it is where we go to get oil.

Scripture seems to connect these two witnesses with the Old and New Testament. Acts 7:44, for example, tells us the Old Testament sanctuary service was a "tabernacle of *witness* in the wilderness." Matthew 24:14 says the New Testament "gospel of the kingdom" is to be a "*witness* unto all nations." One points forward to what Christ would do, the other points back to what he has done. And between them, there is a perfect match! And while we all are witnesses to some extent, Christ himself

---

41. *"We all need to study as never before the parable of the ten virgins. Five of them were wise, and five were foolish. The wise took oil in their vessels with their lamps. This is the holy oil represented in Zechariah [Zech. 4:11-14 quoted]. This representation is of the highest consequence to those who claim to know the truth." Bible Commentaries, vol. 4, p. 1179.*

emphasized the priority of the Bible: "I receive not testimony [witness] from man." "Search the scriptures; for in them ye think ye have eternal life: and these are they which testify of me" (John 5:34,39). The Old and New Testament. Prophecy and fulfillment. Type and antitype. These are the two witnesses–it has to be!

Now if the two witnesses represent the Word of God, then the olive trees must be too. And if the oil flows out of these trees, then we know where to go to get the oil. It comes through Scripture. Does that suggest anything about how we might be able to store up extra oil in our hearts?[42]

THE FIRST GREAT LESSON

Despite the clear and urgent need to have God's Word hidden in the heart as a preparation for the crisis ahead, some have argued against connecting the wise virgins' oil with Scripture, claiming that the oil must be viewed solely as the Holy Spirit.[43] Now without question, the Holy Spirit is intimately involved in the preparation of the wise virgins. The problem comes when we try to *exclude* the Word of God from that process.

---

42. *No where in Scripture are we instructed to "lay up" the Holy Spirit–but we are repeatedly instructed to "lay up" His Word in our hearts!*

43. *The main argument for this, is that the book Christ's Object Lesson links the oil of the ten virgins with the Holy Spirit. However, a careful reading of that chapter also reveals many statements connecting the oil to Scripture. For example: "by implanting in their hearts the principles of His Word, the Holy Spirit develops in men the attributes of God." Through such wise virgins, "the light of His glory–His character–is to shine forth" (p. 414). The foolish virgins, on the other hand, "receive the word with readiness, but they fail of assimilating its principles" (p. 411). And again, "without the Spirit of God, a knowledge of His word is of no avail . . . unless the Spirit of God sets the truth home, the character will not be transformed" (p. 408). Clearly, the focus of this chapter is on the work of the Holy Spirit to write Scripture into the heart and character of the believer.*

Notice the following: "Much is being said regarding the impartation of the Holy Spirit. And by some it is being so interpreted that it is an injury to the churches. Eternal life is a receiving of the living elements in the scriptures and a doing of the will of God."[44] It's not gimmicks and hype that bring revival–it's Scripture. That's where the focus must be! The quotation continues, "These theories were invented by men who have not learned the first great lesson, that God's Spirit and life are *in His word*." God's Spirit is in His word? Amazing! But true.[45] In fact, it is the first great lesson. But it is a lesson we, as God's endtime people, have been slow to learn.

FILL MY CUP LORD

To share in the experience of the wise virgins, we must know experientially where the oil comes from. "All who wait for the heavenly bridegroom are represented in the parable as slumbering because the Lord delayed His coming; but the wise roused themselves at the message of His approach, and responded to the message … They discerned where was *the source of their supply*."[46]

Commenting on the oil again, we read, "this holy oil is poured from heaven in the *messages* of God's Spirit … God is dishonored when we refuse the *communications* that He sends us. Thus we refuse the golden oil that He would pour in to our

---

44. *Selected Messages, vol. II, p. 38-39.*

45. *"The only safety for any of us is to plant our feet upon the Word of God and study the Scriptures, making God's Word our constant meditation . . . The Holy Spirit is in the Word of God." This Day With God, p. 292.*

46. *Signs of the Times, 8/13/1894.*

souls."[47] His messages? His communications? Isn't that talking about Scripture?

Even more clear is the following: "the two olive trees empty themselves in to the golden bowls, which represent the hearts of the living messengers of God who bear the word of the Lord to the people in warnings and entreaties. *The word itself must be as represented, the golden oil* emptied from the two olive trees that stand by the Lord of the whole earth."[48] There it is again. God's Word–in the hearts of His living messengers.

Friends, there is a profound truth here we have missed. The oil is certainly connected with the Holy Spirit. We need to be filled with the Holy Spirit, for it is the work of the Holy Spirit to "take the truth from the sacred page" and "stamp that truth upon the mind."[49] But we have a part too! It is left with us to store up as much of that oil in our vessels as we can. We must invest the necessary effort to fill our heart with God's Word. It's the fuel for the fire–and we're going to need it.

FINAL MOVEMENTS

The final movements are going to be rapid ones–like a string of dominos. And anything could set it off: an economic collapse, a natural disaster, or something supernatural. Suppose, for the sake of illustration, terrorists were to detonate nuclear bombs in three major U.S. cities tomorrow morning. New York, Atlanta, Los Angeles. Wherever. Hundreds of thousands, dead and dying. And threats of more bombs to come. What would happen?

---

47. *Review & Herald, 7/20/1897.*

48. *Manuscript Releases, vol 16, p. 296.*

49. *Healthful Living, p. 300.*

Everywhere people would be arguing our only hope is to get back to God, and *His* protection. That these disasters have come because we, as a nation, have turned our back on God. A crazed effort to legislate religion back into society could easily sweep the country. And with enough public outcry, Washington might be debating religious laws within weeks. The stage would be set for the final apostasy described in Revelation.

As you see the scenes so long foretold taking place before your eyes, you suddenly "wake up" to the shortness of time. You feel constrained to tell everyone the real meaning behind it all. Bible in hand, you knock on your neighbor's door. Where do you start? What do you say? He asks some question you cannot answer. He raises objections you've never heard. You find yourself puzzled and perplexed. You walk home dejected, surprised to discover you don't really know your Bible as well as you thought! Could it happen?

"When the time of trial shall come there are men now preaching to others who will find upon examining the positions they hold, that there are many things for which they can give no satisfactory reason. Until thus tested they *knew not their great ignorance* ... There are many in the church who take it for granted that they understand what they believe, but until controversy arises, they *do not know their own weakness*. When separated from those of like faith and compelled to stand singly and alone to explain their beliefs, they will be surprized to see how confused are their ideas of what they had accepted as truth."[50] Desperately, they will "run to and fro to seek the word of the LORD, and shall not find it" (Amos 8:11-12). Like foolish virgins searching high and low for last minute oil–it is too late.

---

50. *Last Day Events, p. 70.*

AN ALTERNATE ENDING

Now on the other hand, suppose it's not tomorrow morning, but a year from now. Nuclear bombs, three major cities. Catastrophe. A religious backlash and apostasy. Only this time, between now and then, you have made a commitment to begin memorizing Scripture. Yes, it's difficult at first, but you stick with it. In time, it gets easier and soon you are memorizing a couple of verses a week, maybe a verse a day, or even more. In your morning devotions you begin to sense the Holy Spirit highlighting one specific verse after another. You may not even fully understand them all at the time–but you faithfully store them away in your memory. And then the crisis breaks.

You grab your Bible and knock on your neighbor's door. Sitting around his table, you begin to explain the prophecies and how they are being fulfilled all around you. He asks a question and from somewhere a verse flashes into your mind. Just the verse you need. He raises an objection, and then another–and with each one, an exact Scripture comes to mind. Your understanding begins to open. Biblical themes begin to unfold. And you find yourself speaking with a strangely compelling simplicity. Notice the following quotation:

"The servants of Christ are to prepare no set speech to present when brought to trial for their faith. Their preparation is to be made day by day, in *treasuring up in their hearts* the precious truths of God's Word … When brought into trial, the Holy Spirit will bring to their remembrance the very truths that will reach the hearts of those who shall come to hear. God will flash the knowledge obtained by diligent searching of the Scriptures into their memory at the very time when it is needed."[51] It will then be time to "arise, shine; for thy light is come, and the glory of the LORD is risen upon thee" (Isaiah 60:1). The wise virgin's lamps will burst into flame, and shine out into the darkness around them.

CONCLUSION

Friends, there *is* a time of crisis coming. But it will also be a time of apostolic power and glory. It's called the latter rain. And there is an essential preparation–the Word of God. Our vessels must be full. When the unfolding of Bible prophecy becomes so obvious we can no longer evade the reality that the end has actually come–it may be too late to gain the experience we will need. It takes time to internalize the Word. It takes time for the Scripture to do it's work in the heart. To change our thinking. Our will. Our character. We cannot put off that preparation. Delay is deadly. We must start now–*for such a time...*

---

51. *Last Day Events, p. 69.*

The Word Made Flesh
Chapter 7

I thought on my ways,
and turned my feet unto thy testimonies.
Psalms 119:59

The husbandman waiteth for the precious fruit of the earth
and hath long patience for it, until he receive the early
and latter rain. So the Christian is to wait for the fruition
in his life of the word of God ... Our part is
to receive God's Word and hold it fast.[52]

Back in the days when our ministry was just beginning, I remember being invited to conduct a week of prayer at a small church in midstate New York. One night, in the middle of my presentation, a tall, dignified looking gentleman walked into the church. Something about his pinstripe suit and felt-rimmed hat vaguely reminded me of an old gangster movie. As I continued speaking, I noticed his eyes locked onto mine, with an unusual intensity, as though wrestling with some serious question. Then, after the meeting closed, I watched him press forward to the

---

52. *Christ's Object Lessons, p. 61.*

front of the church to speak with me. Not quite sure what to expect, I greeted him.

He proceeded to explain that he had something important to discuss with me, and asked if I would meet with him in his office the next day for a few minutes. I agreed, and soon found myself being chauffeured up to an impressive building complex by one of his staff. Inside, I was ushered straight to the top floor, and then to his "presidential suite." He welcomed me warmly, and we were soon chatting like old friends.

The Lord, it turned out, had been working in his heart, convicting him of the need to do more to advance God's cause. He pulled out a complex chart of interlocking business entities and began to explain what the various parts represented. He then asked my thoughts on his plan. With my limited business background, I couldn't make much sense of it. Some of the entities, evidently, were profit-making ventures that fed money into various other non-profit components. Some pieces in the puzzle were already established, some were in various phases of development, and others were completely future. Some of the components were easily identifiable ministries: publishing, health, education, etc. Others were less clear. I scratched my head wondering what to say.

Suddenly I noticed a small box down in the bottom right corner. It was simply labeled "finishing the work." It caught my attention, and I asked my friend what that box represented. He looked me straight in the eye, and said something I will never forget: "We believe there is still a missing piece to finishing the work, and we are leaving room in our plans for when God reveals it to us." Perhaps you too have thought, there's got to be something we've missed.[53]

SIMPLE MEANS

What we need most is not better evangelistic methods, more persuasive Bible study courses, or a clever new church growth strategy. And it's not technology: the internet, DVD's, satellite, or any other form of media. It's certainly not music and magic! It's not any of the things we tend to invest so much of our energy in.

Notice the following: "The Lord will work in this last work in a manner very much out of the common order of things ... God will use ways and means by which it will be seen that He is taking the reins in His own hands. The workers will be surprised by the *simple means* that He will use to bring about and perfect His work of righteousness."[54]

What could be more simple, than a return to God's Word? To just getting into the Bible, and getting the Bible into us? Actually, is there anything else that *could* do it?

LIGHTNING RODS

The fact is–it is not new methods, or better technologies that we need, but lightning rods. Heaven is already pulsating with plenty of power, bursting with more energy than we can imagine. The problem is there are not enough people through whom that power can flow. People in whom the Word of God

---

53. It should be emphasized that finishing the work will involve more than just one missing piece. "There will be an accumulation of divine agencies to combine with human effort that there may be the accomplishment of the work for the last time. The work will most assuredly be cut short in a most unexpected manner." 1888 Materials, p. 754.

54. Last Day Events, p. 300.

has absolute authority. "The eyes of the LORD run to and fro throughout the whole earth, to show himself strong in the behalf of them whose heart is perfect toward him" (II Chronicles 16:9).

Lightning rods generate no power of their own, they are merely conduits of power. And God is looking for a people who will convey His Word to the world around them, rather than their own ideas and speculations. "For he whom God hath sent speaketh the words of God: for God giveth not the Spirit by measure unto him" (John 3:34). Did you catch that: the Holy Spirit *without measure*?

Listen, when God has a people through whom He can reveal His majesty and might, mere human efforts will quickly pale into insignificance before the awesomeness of an infinite God. But first he has to have that people. Lightning rods.

IN THE BEGINNING

Perhaps looking at it in a slightly different way will help us to capture the real significance of what we have been talking about all along. Notice the profound words John uses to open his gospel: "In the beginning was the Word, and the Word was with God, and the Word was God" (John 1:1). Shocking actually. The Bible we hold in our hands is eternal. And divine. Peter described it as "incorruptible" seed that "liveth and abideth for ever" (I Peter 1:23). And through its pages, he adds, we too can "be partakers of the divine nature" (II Peter 1:4). It's not your typical book.

John continues, "All things were made by him; and without him was not any thing made that was made" (John 1:3). According to Hebrews, "the worlds were framed by the word of God." God "spake, and it was done; he commanded, and it stood fast" (Hebrews 11:3, Psalms 33:9). Clearly, there is creative energy in the Word. In fact, everything that exists is upheld "by the word of his power" (Hebrews 1:3). Every particle in the universe. It's hard to even conceive of such power.

But there's more. "In him [the Word] was life; and the life was the light of men." "That was the true Light, which lighteth every man that cometh into the world" (John 1:4,9). Or as Jesus put it: "the words that I speak unto you, they are spirit, and they are life" (John 6:63). Light and life. Somehow, it is the very essence of Scripture.

Now skip down a few verses: "and the Word was made flesh, and dwelt among us, and we beheld his glory" (John 1:14). This Word that has existed from all eternity, which both created and upholds everything that exists, which is the light and life of men–this Word somehow became embedded in flesh and blood. It was impressed into the very DNA of a man. Jesus Christ. We call this process the *incarnation*. This same Word was somehow captured in paper and ink, in a process we call *inspiration*. An equally miraculous process. We call that book the Bible.

Now here's the point: "Jesus is called the Word of God. He accepted His Father's law, wrought out its principles in his life, manifested its spirit, and showed its beneficent power in the heart. Says John, the Word was made flesh ... *The followers of Christ must be partakers of His experience.*"[55] The Word must become flesh in us? Incredible.

A CRUEL ENEMY

There's an obstacle of course: a cruel enemy. Again from the gospel of John: "the light shineth in darkness; and the darkness comprehended it not." "He came unto his own, and his own received him not" (John 1:5,11). In fact they crucified Him.

---

55. *The Faith I Live By, p. 17.*

Spurred on by a hateful foe who cannot stand the Word of God, the religious leaders committed an atrocity of injustice, nailing those hands ever lifted in blessing to an old rugged cross. They would do it again today, if they could.

Don't underestimate the enemy's hatred of the truths you have been reading. He knows having God's Word in the heart is your only preparation for what is soon to break on our world as an overwhelming surprise. And he will do anything to keep you from obtaining that needed preparation. The battle is real.

Yes, you have an adversary determined to destroy you. And he is full of both malice and cunning. Until this reality sinks in, it will be difficult to resist him. Notice these words:

> *Satan ... is going to and fro in the earth, and walking up and down in it. He is not off his watch for a single moment, through fear of losing an opportunity to destroy souls. It is important that God's people understand this, that they may escape his snares.*[56]

The paragraph goes on to expose his strategy:

> *He is too cunning to come openly, boldly, with his temptations; for then the drowsy energies of the Christian would arouse, and he would rely upon the strong and mighty Deliverer. But he comes in unperceived, and works in disguise.*[57]

---

56. *Testimonies to the Church, vol 1, p. 341.*

57. *Ibid. The passage goes on to point us back to the Scriptures: "The word of God is plain. It is a straight chain of truth, and will prove an anchor to those who are willing to receive it ... It will save them from the terrible delusions of these perilous times."*

To put it differently–the enemy's attacks are usually subtle. They are designed to lull us into complacency. They soften our sense of conviction, dull the edge of urgency. It is the whisper of procrastination: "I'll get to it one of these days..." But that day never seems to come.

Quite frankly, to succeed in internalizing God's Word, we will have to fight through some intense conflict. Expect it. Conquering will require single-minded focus. By God's grace, we must determine to throw off the lethargy Satan casts upon us. You must let nothing stand in your way.

THE HOPE OF GLORY

But honestly, however terrible the foe or fierce the conflict, who would want to turn back now? We stand on the brink of earth's final crisis. Or perhaps, we should say, the final *climax*. The climax to six thousand years of conflict between good and evil. And right now, at this very moment, God is calling sons and daughters for a special purpose. The whole creation "waiteth for the manifestation of the sons of God" when it shall be "delivered from the bondage of corruption into the glorious liberty of the children of God" (Romans 8:19-21). It's our inheritance! "Christ in you, the hope of glory" (Colossians 1:27). Don't you hunger and thirst for it?

If so, determine to get back to the Bible.[58] "The word of Christ" must "dwell in you richly" for "the law of the LORD is perfect, converting the soul" (Psalms 19:7, Colossians 3:16). Through its promises, we can "cleanse ourselves from all filthiness of the flesh and spirit" till we no longer have "spot, or wrinkle, or any such thing" (II Corinthians 7:1, Ephesians 5:26-

---

58. *"It is through the Word that Christ abides in His followers." Desire of Ages, p. 677.*

27). Beholding Christ in the "mirror" of its pages, we will be "changed into the *same image* from glory to glory" (II Corinthians 3:18). A glorious calling indeed.

Actually, what else really compares? Business? Education? Hobbies? Career? Are they even on the same *scale* as oneness with Christ? Paul wrote, we are "called" by the "gospel to the obtaining of the glory of our Lord Jesus Christ" (II Thessalonians 2:14). That's incomprehensible–but thrilling!

Pause for a moment. Still your heart. Listen for God's voice. Isn't He saying something like this: "I'm coming soon. It's time to get ready. You are going to need more of my Word." It's a simple message, but it's one that needs to get out.

CONCLUSION

Even so, I hesitated to put this message into print for years. I wanted to make sure no stone had been left unturned, no careless theological oversight left undiscovered, no imbalance in emphasis left uncorrected. And I might have put it off longer–only the signs of Christ's return are accelerating. And dramatically. Prophetic history is far too advanced. Time is running out. If we are going to do anything to get ready, we better do it now!

Yes, the lateness of the hour calls for our most energetic and determined efforts. It reminds me again of the words quoted at the beginning of the first chapter: "The Lord gives a special truth for the people in an emergency. Who dare refuse to publish it?"[59] We need to give the warning: "prepare to meet thy God" (Amos 4:12). That's why this book is in your hands.

---

59. *Great Controversy, p. 609.*

Which brings the focus back to you. What will you do with the things you have read? It's not just information you realize, it is a call. A call to action. It's a call that could unleash a firestorm of events in your life–if you take it seriously. Satan certainly won't be pleased. But it is also a call to a deeper experience in the most celestial joys imaginable. It's a call back to the Bible. It is a call to glory.

You can accept it, or you can reject it, but you cannot ignore it. You know too much. Like it or not, you've been given an invitation to something very special–*for such a time...*

FAST Missions
Cutting-Edge Tools and Training

Ready to become a Revival Agent? FAST Missions can help! Our comprehensive training curriculum will give you the skills you need to take in God's Word effectively, live it out practically, and pass it on to others consistently.

Eager to start memorizing God's Word? Track #1 will show you how to move from beginner to expert in four key steps.

Ready to explore the secrets of "real life" discipleship? Track #2 zooms in on practical skills for Bible study, prayer, time management, and more.

Want to become a worker in the cause of Christ? Track #3 is designed to give you the exact ministry leadership skills you need to multiply.

For more information, please visit us at:
WWW.FASTMISSIONS.COM

Study Guides

Looking for life-changing study guides to use in your small group or Bible study class? These resources have been used by thousands around the world. You could be next!

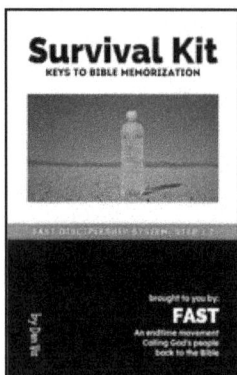

Survival Kit

Want to learn how to memorize Scripture effectively? These study guides will teach you 10 keys to memorization, all drawn straight from the Bible. Our most popular course ever!

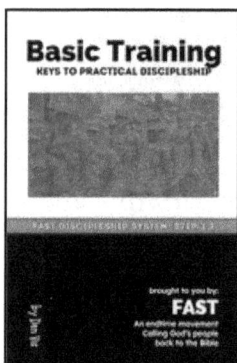

Basic Training

Discover nuts and bolts keys to the core skills of discipleship: prayer, Bible study, time management, and more. Then learn how to share these skills with others. This course launched our ministry!

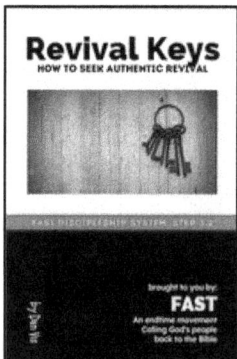

Revival Keys

Now as never before, God's people need revival. And these guides can show you how to spark revival in your family, church, and community. A great revival is coming. Are you ready?

Online Classes

Want to try out some of the resources available at FAST? Here is just a small sampling of courses from among dozens of personal and small group study resources:

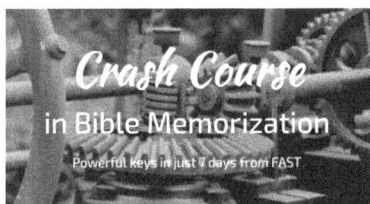

Crash Course
Discover Bible-based keys to effective memorization.
http://fast.st/cc

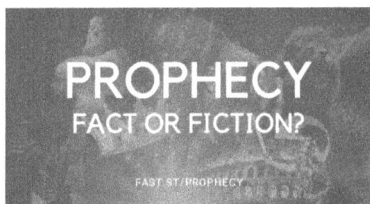

Fact or Fiction
Does the Bible really predict future events? You be the judge.
http://fast.st/prophecy

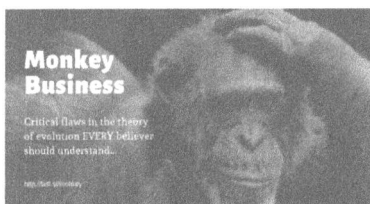

Monkey Business
Find out how evolution flunks the science test.
http://fast.st/monkey

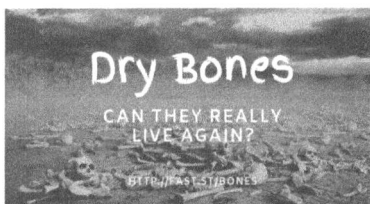

Dry Bones
Want more of God's Spirit? Learn how to pursue revival.
http://fast.st/bones

The Lost Art
Rediscover New Testament keys to making disciples.
http://fast.st/lostart

Digital Tools

FAST offers a number of powerful "apps for the soul" you can use to grow in your walk with God. And many of these are completely free to anyone with an account. Some of these include:

Memory Engine
Our powerful review engine is designed to help ensure effective longterm Bible memorization. Give it a try, it works!

Bible Reading
An innovative Bible reading tool to help you ready through the entire Bible, at your own pace and in any order you want.

Prayer Journal
Use this tool to organize your prayer requests, and we'll help remind you to pray for important requests, on your schedule.

Time Management
Learn how to be more productive, by keeping track of what you need to do and when. Just log in daily and get stuff done.

For more information about more than twenty tools like these, please visit us at *http://fast.st/tools*.

Books

If the content of this little book stirred your heart, look for these titles by the same author.

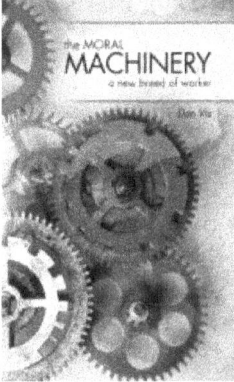

Moral Machinery
Discover how our spiritual, mental, and physical faculties work together using the sanctuary as a blueprint. Astonishing insights that could revolutionize your life!

The Movement
Discover God's plan to finish the work through a powerful endtime movement. Gain critical insights into what lies just ahead for the remnant!

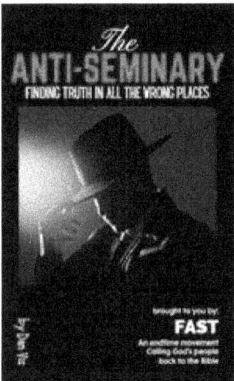

The Anti-Seminary
How a broken young man stumbled his way into the secret place of the most high, and enrolled in the anti-seminary. Finding truth in all the wrong places.